Bos'n Benny and the Saint George Reef Lighthouse

Georgia A. Cockerham

© 2018 Georgia A. Cockerham
colorandwordsbygeorgia.com
All rights reserved.
ISBN-13: 9780989240857
ISBN-10: 0989240851

Dedication

To all past, present, and future keepers of the lighthouse.

Acknowledgment

I extend a warm thank you to Guy Towers and all of the dedicated volunteers who make up the Saint George Reef Lighthouse Preservation Society for their input on the making of this book.

"Well, hello there! My name is Bos'n Benny, and I'm going to tell you about the St. George Reef Lighthouse. You'll learn why the lighthouse was needed and how it was built. You'll also meet my friends, Irish, Tabby, Boris, Perry, Conan, and Sam. We are very pleased that you want to learn about our great lighthouse and the people who have taken care of it. But first, let me tell you a little about myself. I'm a pinniped, or more specifically, a seal. I call the waters around St. George Reef Lighthouse my home.

"Now, about the lighthouse. It was built on Seal Rock, a submerged volcanic mountain a few miles off the shore of Crescent City, California. The caisson is the flat granite surface that is the foundation for the lighthouse tower. At the top of the tower is the great light that communicates to fisherman where the dangerous rocks are so they can steer their boats around the rocks. My friends and I learned about the St. George Reef Lighthouse from our grandparents who saw the lighthouse being built more than 130 years ago. It's a fascinating story that we hope you'll enjoy.

"I'll start by telling you why a lighthouse was needed. A long time ago, before the lighthouse was built, many boats crashed into the reef because the rocks were difficult to see on foggy days and stormy nights. A tower with a light on it was needed to warn ships at sea that large rocks were in the water. The ships could then navigate around the lighthouse and avoid the dangerous rocks. Following one very bad accident on St. George Reef involving a boat called the Brother Jonathan, the United States Congress made the first payment of money to build the lighthouse.

"Well, here is one of my friends. Hello, Irish. I've just started telling these nice people the story of our famous lighthouse. Would you like to help me?"

"Yes, thank you. I'm an Irish setter, and it was my Grandpa Tommy who, with some of the other animals, kept the lighthouse keepers company. There would often be only two to four keepers living at the lighthouse. They'd work there, sometimes for months, before being allowed to leave the lighthouse and return to their home on Point St. George. They'd get lonely, so they loved having me and the other animals around for company. Is that you flying up there, Sam?"

"It's me all right," said Sam the seagull. "I'm enjoying the wind stream with a couple of my friends. Hello everyone. My grandfather soared in the sky watching the lighthouse being built. He told me all about it. The workers needed lots of supplies, including lumber, granite, brick, and cement. The supplies came from Humboldt Bay, Eureka, and McKinleyville. The lighthouse was very difficult to build because the workers had to transfer themselves and supplies from boats in the water to Seal Rock by means of ropes and pulleys.

"A boom was built on the side of the lighthouse for use with a Billy Pugh net or boatswain chair to transfer people and supplies on and off of the caisson."

"Hi there. My name's Tabitha, but my friends all call me Tabby. A lighthouse wouldn't be a lighthouse without a light. I'd like to share what I know about the light.

"Just as light goes through the glass bulb-shaped structure of a light bulb, the light from the lighthouse goes through a glass structure called a Fresnel lens. It is made of many small, carefully cut pieces of glass. The Fresnel lens was a great invention because it allowed the light shining through it to be visible to ships at a much greater distance than could previously be seen with a regular glass lens."

"It's also much easier to care for the light today because we have electricity in the lighthouse. Before electricity the lighthouse keepers used burning oil to keep the light on." Bos'n Benny looked up from where he was swimming. "Is that you up there on the boom, Conan the cormorant?"

"Yes, it is. I like it up here because it's not far from the nest I made in the lighthouse tower window."

"Hello-o-o-o. Let me remind you that bats sleep during the day. Since I can't sleep listening to all of this talk about the lighthouse, can I tell about how the lighthouse keeper saved my grandpa?"

Bos'n Benny smiled. "Sure, Boris. That's a great story."

"Well, my grandpa accidently flew into the side of the lighthouse during a storm, hurting himself pretty badly. One of the keepers found grandpa and helped mend his broken wing so that he could fly again.

"The keeper even made a sign to hang outside of the sleeping space he fixed up for grandpa, warning everyone to be quiet because an injured bat was sleeping."

Bos'n Benny laughed. "I've got another fun story. One day there was a mighty storm causing huge waves to crash against the lighthouse. Grandpa's friend, a sea lion who was swimming near the lighthouse, was lifted up on to a high wave and set down on the caisson. It gave the lighthouse keepers a good laugh."

"Hey there, friends. I'd like to join you with telling this story. I'm Perry, a peregrine falcon, and I'd like to tell how the Coast Guard assumed command of the lighthouse in 1939. They took good care of the lighthouse, making a lot of improvements so that it became a more comfortable place for the lighthouse keepers to live and work. They often caught their dinner by fishing off the rock.

"The Coast Guard watched over the lighthouse for about forty years before giving it to Del Norte County, and allowing the Saint George Reef Lighthouse Preservation Society to make legal decisions for its care and use. You can tell the rest of the story, Bos'n Benny."

"Thank you, Perry," said Bos'n Benny. "I'm very proud of how much my friends know about the famous lighthouse. The Saint George Reef Lighthouse Preservation Society has worked hard to restore the lighthouse, including its important lantern, so that it will continue to be a magnificent feature of our northwest coast and serve the many fishermen who navigate our coastal waters. Today the lighthouse also serves tourists who can take a helicopter ride that lands on the caisson.

"There are lots more stories our grandparents told us, but there's not enough room in one book to tell them all. Before we leave, it's important we let you know that the people who do the restoration work on the lighthouse are always very sensitive to the animals that live on and near it.

"We all hope you've enjoyed our stories and pictures of the historic St. George Reef Lighthouse. Someday maybe you'll come visit the lighthouse and see my friends, and me too. If you do, please wave and shout out a big "Hi!" We love visitors."

QUESTIONS FOR READERS

1.) What is the name of the lighthouse?

2.) What kind of a pinniped is Bos'n Benny?

3.) What is the name of the submerged volcanic mountain on which the lighthouse was built?

4.) What is the primary purpose for building a lighthouse?

QUESTIONS FOR READERS

5.) How did Bos'n Benny and his friends learn about the Saint George Reef Lighthouse?

6.) What are the names of Bos'n Benny's six animal friends?

7.) Why were the animals welcomed at the lighthouse?

8.) For what were the Billie Pugh net and boatswain chair used?

QUESTIONS FOR READERS

9.) What is the name of the light in the lighthouse tower?

10.) How did the lighthouse keeper help Boris the bat's grandpa?

11.) What United States military branch took command of the lighthouse in 1939?

12.) What is the name of the preservation society that oversees care and preservation of the lighthouse today?

QUESTIONS FOR READERS

13.) What is the name of this book's author and illustrator?

14.) What is your favorite part of the story?

DRAW A PICTURE ABOUT YOUR FAVORITE PART OF THE STORY.

ANSWERS TO THE QUESTIONS

- This book is about the Saint George Reef Lighthouse.
- Bos'n Benny is a harbor seal.
- Seal Rock is the name of the submerged volcanic mountain on which the lighthouse was built.
- A lighthouse is built to provide a warning of dangerous rocks to those navigating in waters near and around the lighthouse.
- Bos'n Benny and his friends learned about the lighthouse from their grandparents who told stories about how the lighthouse was built.
- Bos'n Benny's six animal friends are Irish, Tabby, Boris, Perry, Conan, and Sam.
- The animals were welcomed at the lighthouse because they kept the lighthouse keepers company.
- The Billie Pugh net and boatswain chair were used to transport supplies and people between the lighthouse and boats in the water.
- The special light in the tower is a Fresnel lens.
- The lighthouse keeper helped Boris the bat's grandpa by mending his broken wing so that he could fly again.
- The United States Coast Guard took command of the lighthouse in 1939.
- The Saint George Reef Lighthouse Preservation Society currently oversees care and restoration of the lighthouse.
- The name of the author and illustrator is Georgia Cockerham.

www.ingramcontent.com/pod-product-compliance
Lightning Source LLC
Chambersburg PA
CBHW041540040426
42446CB00002B/178